PLANT
Your Words

PLANT Your Words

HEIDI SANDER
& JAMIE NIX

Plants & Poetry

Plant Your Words

Copyright 2022 by Heidi Sander & Jamie Nix

ISBN: 979-8-88627-344-1

All rights reserved.

Book Designer: Jamie Arts

Published by Plants & Poetry House.

The authors greatly appreciate you taking the time to read this work. Please consider leaving a review wherever you bought the book, or telling your friends or blog readers about *Plant Your Words* to help spread the word. Thank you for your support.

Plant Your Words. Copyright © 2022 by Heidi Sander & Jamie Nix. All rights reserved under International and Pan-American Copyright Conventions. This book is sold subject to the condition that it shall not, by way of trade or otherwise, be lent, re-sold, hired out, or otherwise circulated without the publisher's prior consent in any form of binding or cover other than that in which it is published and without a similar condition including this condition being imposed on the subsequent purchaser.

CONTENTS

INTRODUCTION	11
PLANT YOUR WORDS	12
ROOTS OF DOUBT (Sharp-Lobed Hepatica)	16
BECOME A FLOWER (Aster)	20
TURN (Black-Eyed Susan)	24
CARETAKERS (Canada Violet)	28
MORNING SONG (Trillium)	32
LOOKING BACK (Hawkweed)	36
SAVE THE WORLD (Butterflyweed)	40
KOLLMAN ACRES (Wild Apple Trees)	44
WHERE DO THESE WORDS GO? (Yellow Trout Lily)	48
WATCHMEN (Prairie Dropseed)	52

REBIRTH (Indian Grass)	56
ALONE (June Grass)	60
RELEASING (Little Bluestem)	64
BOUNDING (Prairie Cordgrass)	68
PRESSED (Switchgrass)	72
THE LONG JOURNEY	76
CITRON DANCES WITH HONEY (Citrus Limon)	82
BLOSSOM (Dandelion)	86
NATURAL LAWS (Fig Leaf)	90
HEALING (Oregano)	94
AN ODE TO HIBISCUS (Hibiscus)	98
A CUP OF CHARM (Lamb's Quarter)	102
A PLATE OF EGUSI MELON (Egusi Melon)	106
GUT FEELING (Sea Kale)	110
BLACKBERRY FENCE (Blackberry)	114

SMELLS LIKE FREEDOM (Paprika)	118
WORRIED HOURS (Rosemary)	122
SYMPHONY OF SILENCE (Lavender)	126
TRADITION (Date Tree)	130
BREATHTAKING (Mint)	134
TAKE YOU HOME (Aloe Vera)	138
RIAN'S FLOWER (Calla Lily)	142
HOW TO MAKE YOUR OWN SEED PAPER	147
ACKNOWLEDGMENTS	149
ABOUT JAMIE NIX	152
ABOUT HEIDI SANDER	154
ABOUT PLANTS & POETRY	157
ABOUT PATHWAYS TO POETRY	159

To all living beings on this planet.
May we live in harmony with one another.

HEIDI: And to my next generation — you are the future caretakers of this planet: Marlowe, Sidelia, Lucas, Brock, Cooper, Charlotte, and Bentley.

JAMIE: To all my fellow poets & plant people. Thank you for nourishing such important parts in communities.

INTRODUCTION

Welcome to this sanctuary of plants and poetry. These poems explore the depth of relationships, cross-species and cultural interactions, and the natural world creating a collage of poems, thoughts, complaints, musings, sketches, overheard conversations, doubts, dreams, delays, and expectations of our human lives.

Our goal for this slice of magic is to share our most beloved plant companions and enable you to discover yours. Each poem is inspired by a plant from various soil types, climates, and regions.

As this book was a unique collaboration between two poets, we invite you to share your poetry. Each poem is followed by a page open to you for reflection, whether writing a poem or doodling. As this poetry collection touches upon our beautiful planet which we hold so dearly, we hope these spaces for reflection offer you a place to plant your own words and reverence.

As you digest these works and cultivate some of your own, you may keep the pages or restore them in the form of seed paper. After you have absorbed this collection, you will find instructions toward the back of this book on how to plant your words and make your own seed paper. See "Plant Your Words: How To Make Your Own Seed Paper. This can become an annual ritual where you harvest seeds directly from a seedhead in your garden.

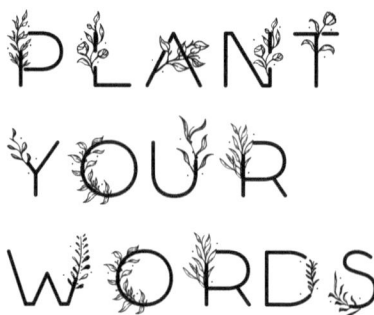

PLANT YOUR WORDS

Plant your words

      here

on this page,
on your lips
in the garden
of your mind

where thoughts blossom
grow in the dappled shadows,
the moist earth of tomorrow.

Seed life with your words,
sprout your dreams
cultivate possibilities.

Water these pages of your life,
the pale forearm of this line
burrowing through the soil.

REFLECTION

Where does your imagination live? Is it in nature?
Write about where you find it.

Date: /   /

Roots of Doubt

(SHARP-LOBED HEPATICA)

Close to the cool earth,
a depth of purple
in its cupped petals,

so much light
rising from the murky earth,
so much life
lapping up the darkness
so much hope growing
from the cold hand of winter

and I think:
that seed of faith
is always there
wrapping its roots
around our doubt.

REFLECTION

What do the changes of the season mean to you?
Are you in awe of spring?
Do you hibernate in winter?

Date: /   /

BECOME A FLOWER
(ASTER)

Live another life
turn words back to earth
become a flower.

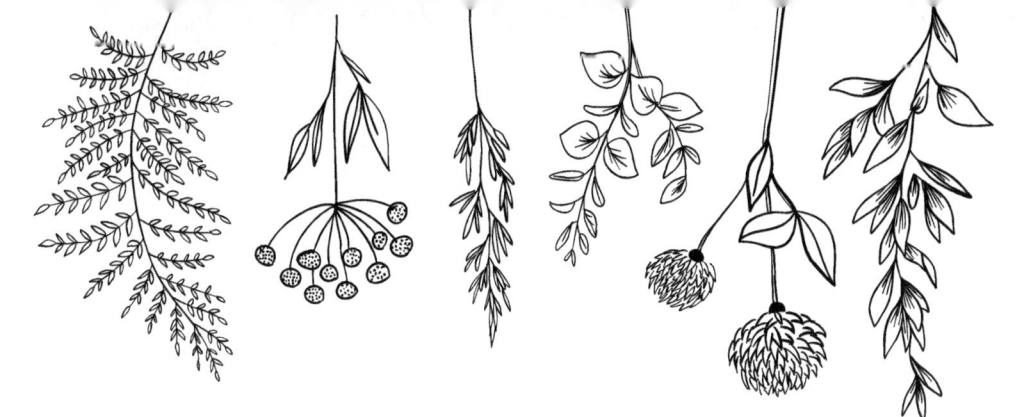

REFLECTION

If you were to turn one moment around in your life, what would it be? What is the one thing you want to do with this life of yours?

Date: /   /

TURN

(BLACK-EYED SUSAN)

Flowers turn their petals
to the blossom of the sun
they know it's time to shine,
don't ask how long they have,
    the sun will tell them,
    a darkening sky
    cooler winds.

They live for this day,
without questioning
without worrying.

They are our teachers
if we only take time to watch,
to listen to their silent poems.

REFLECTION

How can you live in the moment today?
What have you learned from that?

Date: /   /

CARETAKERS
(CANADA VIOLET)

For Brilla

A delicate violet planted herself
in the back garden,
underneath the rock,
reaching for the tiny paws
folded over one another
when we buried you there.

We dug the hole so carefully,
laid your resting body with
flower petals, words of love,
your favourite toy.

We left the violet
among the irises we planted,
wild and free as you once were,

we don't own this backyard
this garden,
or anything at all.

29 | PLANT YOUR WORDS

REFLECTION

Is there a particular piece of the earth that you love? What is your role as its caretaker and how do you protect it?

Date: /   /

MORNING SONG
(TRILLIUM)

You,
are a song,
that opens and closes
with the light

rises and falls
in the wind,
laps up
the dew

calls out
to search
for the light
we cannot see.

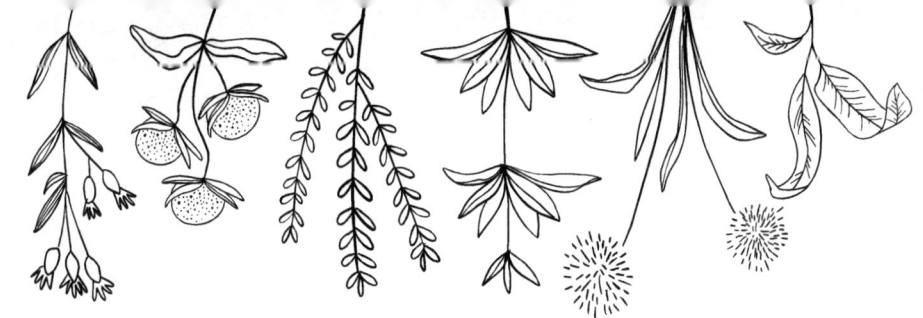

REFLECTION

Nature holds so much we cannot see.
What plant do you wait for when spring emerges?
What do you have faith in even if you don't see it?

Date: /   /

35 | PLANT YOUR WORDS

Looking Back
(Hawkweed)

In the wide gardens of the prairie,
bees collect nesting materials,
then dip and turn on grass flowers,
pollen covering thin legs,
an endless wave flowing to the hive,
the centre of their Universe.

On one blossom, a bee on its back
kicks its legs in the air,
I lift a leaf till it grabs hold,
then place it right side up.
For a long while it doesn't move;
opens its wings once, closes them.

Was I too late?

Then wings buzz and lift into the air,
it flies to the next flower, joins the river of bees.

*How often do you look back
and think of your life?*

REFLECTION

Is there a place in nature's garden where you go to reflect? When you reflect on your life journey so far, what was the one moment that has made it all worthwhile?

Date: / /

SAVE THE WORLD
(BUTTERFLYWEED)

What I dream of
on a harsh winter's day
what floats to my mind

is this garden of light
long breath waiting
underneath the hard earth,
lifeblood frozen
in the branches and vines,
this verdant green
that will save our world.

REFLECTION

Write about your relationship with nature. Are you in awe of it's power? Appreciative for its serene environment? What are you doing to save this beautiful miraculous planet?

Date: /   /

KOLLMAN ACRES
(WILD APPLE TREES)

I sit under the bent roof of the apple orchard, branches curved to blades of grass, a thick layer of fruit blocking the sun's warm fingers. Here at the base of the gnarled trunk, my view is through a door of leaves, across time,

to the row along the meadow, nurtured during the 1930s drought when each child woke up extra early on the farm and carried a bucket of water to every tree.

In the distance, an apple drops, joining those on the green floor, the ones destined for the mouths of rabbits, deer, or the lips of moist earth. They turn their red bodies, ears pressed to the ground, listening.

Beneath my feet, trees talk to one another, a long string of filaments woven throughout this meadow. Theirs is a friendship, a symbiosis forged for millions of years. Deep in the layers of earth they share sugars, trade resources, send danger warnings.

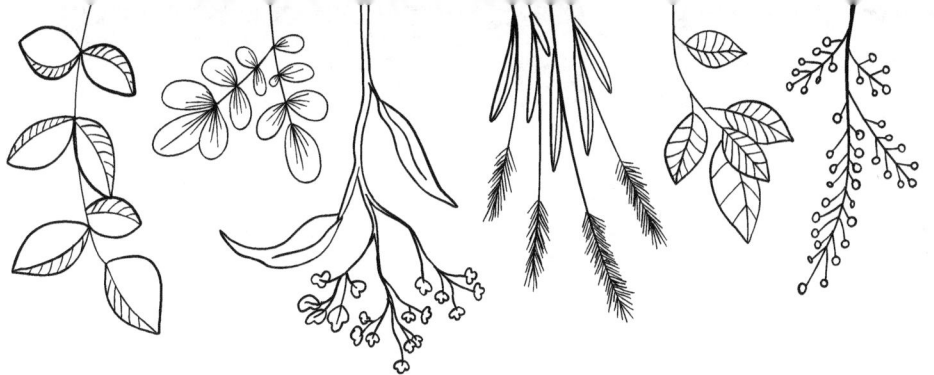

What did they say to the little child with the bucket? *One day, your daughter will live here, raise her children, continue to care for this land. Her horse will graze at our feet.*

REFLECTION

Do you ever wonder about the lives that have lived on a spot of land? What stories the trees and plants could tell...

Date: /   /

WHERE DO THESE WORDS GO?
(YELLOW TROUT LILY)

Where do these words go
once they're written?

What happens to a thought
when spoken?

Beyond this page,
flowers push through
moist shell of earth,
leaves turn and tumble,
petals shake seeds to the wind.

the moon blossoms in the sky
stars climb into its pocket
and these words remain

      here.

REFLECTION

If there were one word, one poem, one piece of writing that would remain beyond your lifetime, what would you want to say?

Date: /   /

WATCHMEN
(PRAIRIE DROPSEED)

It was late summer

wandering in the open grasses

these watchmen of the prairie

walked into the cool of

a widespread storehouse

tall green milkweed

dense blazing-star

giant spreadwing dragonfly

five-lined skink

they are all rare,

like you

habitats destroyed

searching for safety

afraid of machinery

destroying habitat

till the earth stands empty

Still, these watchmen

trust us to enter.

when I brushed up against them,

the wind shook,

opened their pale green coats

their bodies,

of cilantro and gold

dwarf lake iris

white-fringed orchid

short-winged green grasshopper

cerulean warbler

threatened, endangered,

population in decline

like you

hiding from us

barreling through meadows

eradicating life

under embers of stars

open their mossy green house

REFLECTION

Is there a wild place that you leave untouched when you enter? Do you feel that you're entering someone else's home?

Date: /   /

REBIRTH
(INDIAN GRASS)

Sometimes I live
like Indian grass
rising and falling
with the wind,
    boundless.

Fires don't stop them
nor do bison,

only man.

But they sharpen the edge of their blades,
toss their pollen to the wind,
they return under broad sky,
infinite and calm
they transcend, regrow.

REFLECTION

Is there a time in your life when you felt defeated?
How did nature inspire you to carry on?

Date: /   /

ALONE

(JUNE GRASS)

You flower early on the rooftop,
opening your silver-green seed heads
to the sun
till they tan golden brown,
then,
purple,
the colour of royalty
as you break your fruit open
drop grains for the birds,
scan the horizon
for signs of your prairie grass
brothers and sisters -
they are brooms and brushes
porridge and bread,
growing in golf course roughs,
open wilds, as high as 2,480 metres.

They are cut down for pasture,
cleared for development,
    you are safe, they tell you,
    alone on the rooftop.

61 | PLANT YOUR WORDS

REFLECTION

Are there times you feel alone among your family and loved ones? Do you find comfort in nature?

Date: /   /

RELEASING
(LITTLE BLUESTEM)

Every winter
they wrap their dainty claws
around your slender red stems
orange bronze fireworks
against the snow.

You loosen your nougat shoulders,
lift fuzzy white fingers,
open your seeds to them.

This emptiness contains
what you need:
    A new beginning.

REFLECTION

Do you live in tune with nature? Do you turn a new leaf each year? Shake loose the past and start fresh?

Date: /   /

BOUNDING
(PRAIRIE CORDGRASS)

Along the railroad tracks
a rabbit's bent body
swallows the stars.

Perhaps he left
the protective cover
of the flat emerald blades,
thought the train's whistle
was the moon calling him
and with one leap,
bounded into
a warm pool of light.

Isn't everyone waiting
to break free of the darkness?

REFLECTION

Is there a weight you want to break free from?
Do you find that release in nature?

Date: /   /

PRESSED
(SWITCHGRASS)

Once, it grew in vast swaths across North America fields,
just as the passenger pigeon once filled the sky.

Don't just turn it into a renewable bioenergy crop.
Don't just press it into fuel pellets to heat homes.

Walk into the open meadows, where the European
settlers are plowing the tall stems under to grow corn.

Stand among them as cattle farmers from Saskatchewan to
Mexico, replace it with fescue for hay.

Now lie down in the switchgrass,
stare through the green window
into the swirling sky.

> *Is it only once we prove ourselves useful*
> *that we are valued?*

REFLECTION

Do you question your self worth?
Do you question the value nature holds?

Date: /   /

THE LONG JOURNEY

It's a long journey
to find a place in this world.

Spring wildflowers know this,

burrowing their way
through darkness
till cool rains
seep into their skin.

They anchor themselves

deep in the earth, pushing

toward an unknown future,

summoned by a primal voice

deep inside
that whispers:

>*Live.*

>*Grow.*

Each flower makes
the difficult journey,

before the tree canopy

closes with thick foliage.

Trilliums cover the hillsides

their long pale fingers
rising from three broad leaves

like freshly fallen snow.

Mayapples unfurl

partially opened umbrellas

hiding a pale moon
under wings of green.

Although their life is brief,

each morning the moon petals

open their eyes,
lift their faces to the sun.

Standing among them,

my bare feet are drawn

through dry leaves

raking through

memory's dark cave

I'm summoned back

warm fingers
of light
lifting me off the ground.

REFLECTION

Is there a spring ritual you perform each year?

Date: /   /

CITRON DANCES WITH HONEY
(CITRUS × LIMON)

honey honey honey honey
proliferating, precipitating moisture
prepping my pretty pores with perspiration

swindled Neutrogena with
vitamin   B-6, Calcium
potassium   iron   Sodium
Copper   Zinc

drizzling a dewy delicacy onto my cheeks
the sweet citron serum

a lemon, a connoisseur of sorts,
flushing out all engendered toxins
an honest fruit,
a great deal of probity

an empirical provider of vitamin C and B
Bolstering polemical pimples, wrestling wrinkles
a small remedy for a weary evening

such serious juice
sabotaging, subverting one's blackheads
a lauded lemon corroborated

with a nectar and here we are...
ruminating

*Is the marriage of our fruit and nectar the
key to our problems of the modern world?*

REFLECTION

Write a poem about the synergy between two living things. Plants, herbs, nectars, and humans. What is sacred about this union, this bond?

Date: /   /

 BLOSSOM
(DANDELION)

a once-was weed
no longer obsolete
a benign blossom gone good

From root to flower
this dandelion bleeds nutrition
a professor of plants that sit beside the garden

loaded with vitamins, minerals and fiber
this perplexing pedagogue peruses our cups for punctilious prizes
some sweet, creamy, particularly easy

this pundit perennial will bud
discernibly, diligently
plodding, prodding you with blazing strings called petals

a flower head of delight
a lenient line waiting its turn for someone lucky to find it.

PLANT YOUR WORDS

REFLECTION

Dandelions have a lot of medicinal and helpful properties. What is something in your life that has many uses? How do you discover it?

Date: /   /

NATURAL LAW
(FIG LEAF)

Emulated from a sweet tooth long ago
The fig leaf is a prudent prophetic piece of the past

A transcendental transitory
Mitigating the pressures between our psyches
This boiling bowl of leaves is a cup of contemporary art

This tree brews foliage, she knows no boundaries
Her fruit drops at the first site of terracotta
Dry and resilient, she scales buildings, builds towns

Fig is the finite fruit of all people with a bias to the desert
She is the jewel of our evening snacks
Her sugars speak to our gut and draw a declaration on our brain

Fig is the mother tree of our natural laws
She writes policy for microbes that survive
She is the passport we lost when we traded
her ripeness for newtons, containers

Her sweet life is bound to the coasts
So, when you see her, take a leaf for a souvenir

Because her sap will not last forever.

Our trees are our relations,
how can we pay our respects?

REFLECTION

Write about one of your favorite trees. Why do you admire it? When did you first meet this species? What does it look like? Where does it live?

Date: /   /

HEALING
(OREGANO)

Anti Anti Anti
Biotic
Oxidant
Good for us They / She / Her
Gut Health – hello

N a t u r a l

anti anti anti
inflammatory
pain
cancer
Oregano

Oh reg who knows
Zayt al zatune
Oil from little angels that sit in trees
They will drop on the ground
once it is ready for you and me

Pick her leaves her out to dry
She may not like to be left alone
so put her in the sun outside,
but only after she swims in the oil inside the jar
She will be ready once
and for most diminishing all our inside scars
Oh reg who knows

REFLECTION

Write about an herb you use often.
How do you use it? What does it taste like?

Date: /   /

An Ode to Hibiscus
(Hibiscus Rosa-Sinensis)

Dear Hibiscus,
you sit outside my window and stretch your limbs towards
bags of skin that transport secrets

Red, right?

Meddling your aroma,
I create ecstasy that blooms Botox onto my face
Embroiled with acne,
demanding pink points escape from the basement of my lip

I did not know you were coming until I walked into the living room
I witnessed you sitting on the counter
Petals folded, nothing short of a revelation

Subsided & waiting for the sun
You could cover the whole block if I let you
On my walk I pretend I do not see the neighbor's shrubs,
of this habitual flower

"They do not belong to you."

We wait until nightfall after iftar
when I know families sit devouring the dinner table
I just want one...each night

This then turns into a deciduous mountain
Of gooey goodness that turns this quagmire of pimples,
these perennials, into a soft piece of paper

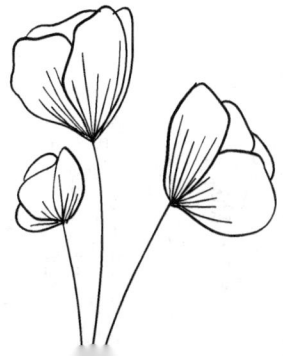

REFLECTION

Write a poem about someone who inspires you to seek new opportunities. What plant do they remind you of and why? Do they bloom best in summers hibiscus, or fall?

Date: /   /

A CUP OF CHARM
(LAMB'S QUARTER)

A sacred trade between tribes
Petals as currency
A steaming cup of Lamb's Quarter tea

Treats stomach aches and diarrhea

Crushed, crumbled, creased, conformed
Dogeared, crocodile tungs

Blades of smooth trilateral relief
Cushions of anti-inflammatory
A rouse to the skin
Farewell to burns, itches, and uncomfortable stitches of dermis.

Stew your pot
Break your leaves
Pour yourself a cup of Lamb's Quarters Tea

* One warning – this plant contains high levels of sodium.

REFLECTION

Lambs Quarter is a powerful plant. How did you use it? Have you used any plants that provide deep knowledge and power? Did you share this knowledge with anyone else?

Date: /   /

A PLATE OF EGUSI MELON
(CUCUMEROPSIS MANNII)

A hidden, treasured, pear colored melon
Drips a superlative seed oil

sorcery of antioxidants and minerals
       vitamin E B-carotene potassium calcium minerals
       magnesium phosphorus iron zinc

Regulating our blood pressure the way
Our heart pumps and slows at the sight of
Our most loved

plant foods friends foreshadowing our chest's content
       fatty acids cholesterol-free linoleic acid
       preventing the devil's disease

Egusi holds space for every coronary artery
Disciples of Scholar Town swear by it, Baylin Wijendran Hayes

anti-rheumatic anthelmintic hydrogogue
      a remedy for pieces of melanin
      the medicine for skin infections

A closet of confectionery places
      Yet even this body of fruit
          And all her seeds are used in the treatment of diabetes.

raw, ripe, an Egusi melon uncut,
sliced on the hottest summer's day

REFLECTION

Certain fruits only grow in certain parts of the world. Write about a time you experienced a new food. Who was it with? What did it look and smell like?

Date: / /

GUT FEELING

(SEA KALE)

It is not wrapped in plastic or glued to the supermarket shelf
No produce section, biased against spinach and lettuce
but seeded deep along the Mediterranean coast

Sea Kale offers bouquets of White bulbs,
pinches of   vitamin C
Fiber locked in each crevice of green stalk

The five leaves discount for all green fingers
Interested in oil harvested from seeds
A free detox grown along the Atlantic

Our monthly cycle invites all the gifts of fresh
                                                    Iodine
Hormone Regulation on tap
Drizzled with a light vinaigrette.

Sea Kale baked, crisp scents of morning
Tastebuds bread in the evening
A delicate boost of clean   immunity

This radical state-of-the-ocean's art
Energy meets nature's specialty with

                        Crambe Maritima

REFLECTION

Think of an element earth, water, fire, air.
Write about this element in different dimensions.
Use all five senses.

Date: /   /

BLACKBERRY FENCE
(RUBUS FRUTICOSUS)

6 feet spruce trees cut and carved into privacy fences
barricaded on the perimeter around Bentonville homes
Yet, our neighborhood,
blessed with blackberry guards

Bouncers of Bella Vista, AR.
Berries bloomed into the oblivion
Each thorn stabbed my exhausted sweaters

Shepherds of the woods
Transformers rose hazelnut bushes back from the grave
These tart chameleons, rubies burned into new jewels

From scarlet
      burgundy
           Russian violet
                  raisin
                        eggplant
                            plum
                                sangria
                                    To the finest wine

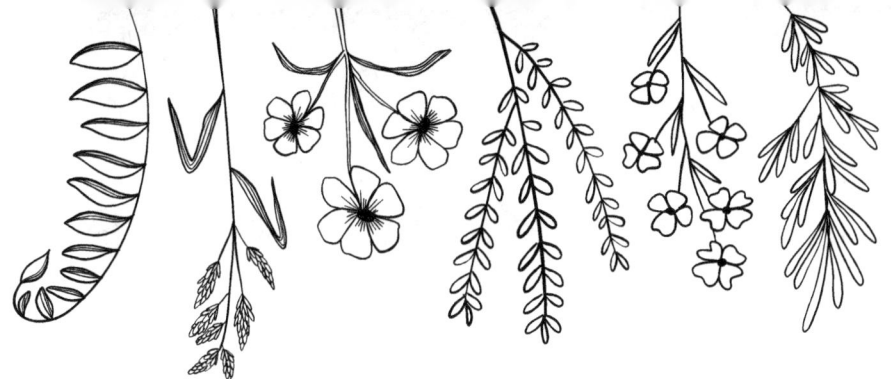

a metamorphosis of sweetmeat and pungent pleasure
4 feet tall branches, slim limbs perched around the house
Blackberry harvest situated between the July heat of August summer
Just in time for a remedy, a banquet of blackberry ice-cream

REFLECTION

Write a memory of the first time you can remember feeling one with nature. How old were you? Were you playing in the woods, picking flowers, climbing a tree?

Date: /   /

SMELLS LIKE FREEDOM
(PAPRIKA)

What color is paprika?
Native to tropical areas of the Western Hemisphere
      Mexico
      Central America
      South America
      and the West Indies
Orange? A shade of sunset red that I know to be paprika
Rich in antioxidants, vitamins, and minerals
      Vitamin A
      Calcium
      Iron
      Potassium
      Vitamin B6
      Vitamin E

Crushed, meddled pepper from a plant 1.5-2' ft tall
With heels buried in silt loam, high-quality
Well-draining soil, now a perfume…
that stains your manicure all through dinner.

Paprika is made of particles made into mountains of fresh air,
Paprika smells like a hot afternoon, a cool dawn morning.

Paprika is not brown, burgundy, but electric
Soft, loud, abundant
                                      Paprika looks like freedom.

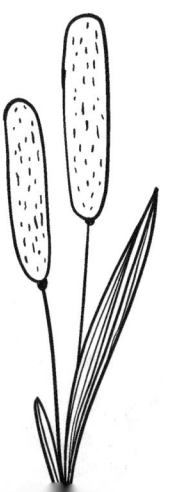

REFLECTION

Write about a time when you felt free, unannounced, full, abundant like a basket full of all your favorite fruits after a high-yielding summer.

Date: /   /

WORRIED HOURS
(ROSEMARY)

The princess herb to the pine tree
Native to the Mediterranean
A rose given to Mary, whose leaves fall
And breed fresh oil and raw medicine
                          increase blood circulation
                          hair growth
Uncured sources of antioxidants and anti-inflammatory compounds,
                          boosting the immune system
                          improving blood circulation
A cognitive stimulant, catering to our memory
Her leaves become pages in the photobook of our dreams
                          Improving our intuition
                          Alertness of the sun
                          Intelligence of the moon
                          Focused on the stars
Rosemary was born to replace our worried hours
She burns and purifies the air in which we breath
Reminding us that we were all just once
Seeds

*Ingestion of large quantities of rosemary may
 cause intestinal irritation, kidney damage and/or toxicity.*

REFLECTION

Think about a plant that reminds you of a loved one. Why? Write a poem about the relationship between this plant and your person.

Date: /   /

SYMPHONY OF SILENCE
(LAVENDER)

A son of the Lamiaceae family
Believed to be native to the Mediterranean
                          Middle East
                          India
With a historical dialogue reaching as far back as 2,500 years
In the ancient universe, lavender was holy, revered
Pebbles for pedals, fields full of fresh foliage

Lavender was once purple gold
Perfumes of release, cologne masking anxiety
Brewed into potions for the common wom(man)
A sacred elixir that rewarded a symphony of silence
At harvest, this flower and her music, a radio of bees

What shall we do when the pollinators no longer work for free?

REFLECTION

Write a poem about a beautiful scent.
Where did you discover this smell?
What does it remind you of?

Date: /   /

TRADITION

(DATE TREE)

Behind every date palm is 1,000 weddings
100 dinners, Two lovers, 2,000 lbs. of protein balls
Centuries of tradition

A trunk evolved and revered by old towns
Behind every date palm is 1,000 weddings
100 dinners, Two lovers, 2,000 lbs of protein balls
Centuries of tradition
Native to
        Saudi Arabia
        Iran
        Iraq
        Morocco
These trees breathe in warm climates
        Canary Islands
        Mexico
        California
        Florida
        Arizona
A trunk evolved and cherished by old towns
The date sanctified my marriage
Some share a slice of red velvet cake on the edge
Of silverware, two hands
But the date, whole, giving, robust

A promise of the ages, stock and seedling
This fruit is devotion, a bond between human and palm

REFLECTION

Write a poem about a plant that you use for ceremonial purposes. If you do not have one, what is one that you have heard about before? Are there plants that you wish to learn more about? Why?

Date: /   /

BREATHTAKING
(MINT)

A dream of the past
the plant of the future
She will take over the garden

welcome the bees
With water to go around
she sits well with tea

Mint is one to consume
Override
so often invade

The master of mosquito deterrent
A warrior of our skin
Mint is careful, sensitive, and all the while

breathtaking

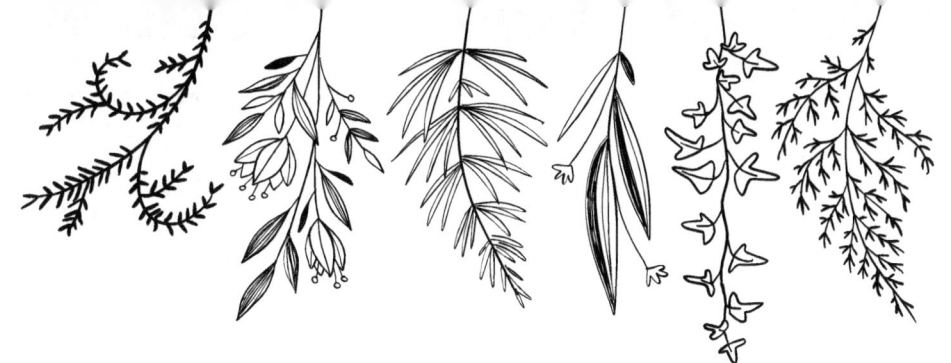

135 | PLANT YOUR WORDS

REFLECTION

Write about a fresh food you bought outside of the supermarket? Have you ever? Have you grown your food? Write a poem about consuming a favorite fruit or vegetable straight from the earth?

Date: /   /

TAKE YOU HOME
(ALOE VERA)

Olivera
Hayaatii My life My darling
I am finally here
To take you home
I hope this is clear
We will water you deep
and play in the sun
We will spend all-day
until the time is done
You soothe
Moisturize
You help our barely soft skin
Your mother is kind
Sharing her tiny little limbs

REFLECTION

Write about a plant that has healed some piece of you? Your spirit, your mind, your body.

Date: /   /

RIAN'S FLOWER
(CALLA LILY)

2-6 hours of sun
Shaded green and white leaves
Flowers with patches and ruffles of pink

Water well, check often
Dry weather must come
As the soil has needs!

Always check, she may bloom early
Spring through the summer
The time has come
Find her a place in a field, a garden
Of all that feels holy

Her roots are grateful for your attention.

She reaches for the strongest roots
And only finds the stars, clear company
A crown that shines beneath the balcony

She plants each eyelash, falling like seeds
Planting them exactly where they belong
Mapping out her nights, waking to rise a new dawn

The rain is sometimes mistaken for a storm
But when it passes, the sun shines brighter than ever before
This calla lily is a friend of a lifetime

REFLECTION

Write about a plant that you are grateful for. How does it affect you? Who introduced you?

Date: /   /

PLANT YOUR WORDS: HOW TO MAKE YOUR OWN SEED PAPER[1]

Step 1: Gather Paper, Tear, Put into Blender

After you have written your poems and reflections in these pages, choose which ones you would like to release, draft, or let go. Tear the paper from this book and gather the paper. You can also include newspaper, egg cartons, and tissue paper. After you have your paper, tear it into small pieces. Take your blender and fill it halfway with the tiny, torn pieces of paper.

Step 2: Pour in Warm Water, Blend into a Smooth Pulp

Next, pour warm water over the paper in the blender. Completely, fill the blender. Blend the water and pieces of paper on low speed for ten seconds. After ten seconds, increase the speed for thirty seconds. After this is done, there should not be any visible paper flakes. Just mush.

---

1   Skylar Christenson, Nature's Seed 2012

Step 3: Stir in Seed, Strain

Think about which kinds of seeds you would like these poems and reflections to pair with. What will your poems bloom as? Once you have decided, add your seeds. Sprinkle a teaspoon of flower, herb, or vegetable seeds into the mixture and stir them in. DO NOT BLEND! Stir them only. Choose a seed blend that is compatible with the climate where you will plant the seed paper. After you have added the seeds, pour the mixture into a strainer. Drain as much water as possible. You can use a spoon press the mush and drain the water.

Step 4: Spread Pulp, Flatten, Dry

Lay out a cloth on a flat surface. Dump the pulp onto the fabric and spread the pulp over the cloth. You can create any shapes you want but spread the mixture as thin as possible. The lighter the paper, the quicker it will dry. Use a sponge to soak up more water. After the pulp has dried on one side, turn it over dry the other side. Once both sides are dry, your seed paper is ready for use.

Create your own seed paper for future poems, love notes, letters, recipes, remedies, and reflections. Seed paper can also be used for invitations or mixed media.

ACKNOWLEDGMENTS

HEIDI SANDER

My heartfelt gratitude to you, the reader. You have read this book and must be a kindred spirit in caring for this beautiful planet. Thank you for sharing that love.

I have written books where proceeds went toward environmental projects and I am thrilled to work with Plants and Poetry House whose work is so important for our earth — I am grateful that they share in the vision of this book. My deep appreciation also to Jamie Arts for the cover design and interior layout which artistically weaves together this entire collection.

If there is someone who encapsulates the love and nurturing of this planet it is my sister, Renate. She is the one person in my life who has dedicated her heart to protecting this planet, from maintaining her country home as a nature preserve, fostering a city pollinator sanctuary, and mentoring hundreds of environmental students. She is an inspiration and someone I admire and look up to for her tender love and nurturing for those who have no voice — the spiders she rescues, the plants she nurtures, the birds she calls to.

My deepest thanks to my fellow poet and co-creator Jamie Nix. This is the first time I have collaborated with another poet on a collection and it was such a rewarding experience exchanging ideas and letting our words grow. The creative flow we had changed the initial concept for this book into one that is much deeper and more interactive for the reader. It's been a special experience sharing my raw poetry with you.

My innermost thanks and appreciation to John for supporting me in my creative pursuits, especially all my years of writing — your understanding, encouragement and love carry me during these times. You, are the poetry in my life.

In my early years, it was my parents who introduced me to the wonder and adventure of the natural world, from outdoor walks to evening stargazing. Thanks Mom for the annual excursions to our fort in the woods, swims in the pond and nurturing my reverence for the wonder of nature. Thanks Dad for afternoons at the farm, rock collections, and teaching me frog calls. Thanks also to my grandparents whose daily lifestyle, from recycling to gardening — set a solid foundation for living in harmony with the natural world.

And deep gratitude to my dear friend, Heather, for her daily encouragement and support. And finally, thanks to all those who have been a part of my growth as a writer: Carol Jankowski, Jim Reid, Nancy Rotozinski, Joyce Eichholz, and Edith Janke.

I gratefully acknowledge the following publications, in which poems from this book have previously appeared, sometimes in slightly different form:

Plant People, An Anthology of Environmental Artists: The Long Journey

As I started this book, I would like to leave the last thought for mother earth — my childhood playground, my inspiration and solace throughout the years. May you continue to breathe for us, sustain us, and may we grow into that same reverence for you.

JAMIE NIX

For my mothers, my grandmothers, great grandmothers, and all of the women before me who cradled a space of reflection, growth, expansion, and new beginnings. You have taught me how to see the world through a lens hyper-focused on species outside of myself. From plants, animals, to tiny microbes that build soil networks beneath my feet. I am forever grateful for your wisdom and intention when I roam around this planet.

When I would be in a frightening, dark place, my grandmother, Angela Robinson, always told me to walk outside, put my barefoot on the earth, touch the bark of a tree, reground myself. She passed away this year with ALS, but I still feel her when I roam the garden or walk down the city streets, scaling the citrus trees on Victory Avenue. My mother, Sunny Lane, would instruct me to listen to my breath and observe my environment, is it safe? Is it full? I used to wonder what she meant by safe and full, but as I got older I began to realize she meant me — as the environment. Am I safe? Am I full? Am I surrounded by people and places that bring me joy?

This book was written during a time when I was indeed both, safe and full. Safe in my own head and full of new poems, opportunities, people, and places. One of those people being, Heidi Sander, a co-creator, for this book, Plant Your Words. Heidi has been an inspiration for me as I continue this journey as a writer. Thank you for this experience, Heidi.

I would also like to thank my dear friend, Leslie Walker. My reflection, my soul sister, my teacher, my friend. Thank you for all you do for our growing village.

And to my husband, thank you for your constant support, encouragement, and deep love. You embrace me for all that I am and allow me to be my full self.

ABOUT JAMIE NIX

Jamie Nix (she/her) cultivates her passion for storytelling, connecting communities, edible landscapes, and water and soil restoration. She navigates the boundaries between poetry, prose, and creative nonfiction. She writes about the depth of relationships, cross-cultural interactions, and the natural world creating a collage of thoughts, complaints, musings, sketches, overheard conversations, doubts, dreams, delays, expectations, remedies, revelations, and explorations.

Her current work includes organizing the Plants & Poetry Journal, which plants a tree or type of vegetation in a Food Forest in Bella Vista, Arkansas. She aims to partner with other poets and authors, nonprofits, schools, zines, and journals on literacy, language learning, and agroforestry initiatives. You can connect with her at www.plantsandpoetry.org or via email jamiemarienix@gmail.com i used to believe i was a sunflower, sitting on a balcony. i soon discovered my dirty finger nails. i was never a flower. just a plantee. roots digging in my cuticles. not a rose. not anything that smells sweet, but i was a seed. saved. only sovereign when food was scarce and my cries for water became clear. a seed. planted in new soils. i am two weeks waiting. patience in our cool corners. headbands that soak the oil from my scalp. 1 pair of saved gold earrings. i am three sisters. A shed below my mothers yard. a stack of over used credit cards. soft sandals, short boots. barefoot. books i cannot complete. i am the paper hoarding pundit. a montessori mind. the porch whisperer. the marble of my city. A toddler of payne's holler. the sylvia, the silvie. silva. i am the spirit of the wood. i am pieces of the willow tree, as i climb back into the forest of our people. A listener. Of the question. i am a hand. hands. headstands. the sky on tuesdays, the air on wednesdays, the fire on fridays, the water, and the earth. i am the libra, balancing. prayers that hang along my window. i am the collage of polaroids. bulletin boards, magnetic words. the orange scarf on the weekends. i am the song that reminds me to read. telefone in the background. i am the four leaved clover i created with two crops. i am the sailboat that will be here when you come up for air. parked just the under the atlantic. i am the dictionaries of languages i do not speak yet. i am the tea soaked in honey. i am a slice of bread with zameta. sometimes peach jam. jamila. woh-thee-yoh. jam. jame-o. hbiba. madame. hayaati. baby i am black coffee with cold milk. cafe noir. i am lavender on your temples. i am burning our old leaves. i am the weaver, the writer, the wanderer, the seeker. the researcher underneath. a molecular meditator. perhaps i am not a flower. i am a garden. A Piece Of It.

JAMIE NIX

ABOUT HEIDI SANDER

Award-winning poet, Pushcart Prize nominee, and best-selling author, Heidi Sander's (she/her) poems have appeared in literary journals, anthologies, and multiple artistic collaborations. She is the founder of "Pathways To Poetry", a multimedia online program that helps emerging and established poets develop their writing, publish their poetry, and promote their work.

Her award-winning poem, "How We Live On", is being developed into a short film that will be touring film festivals. The poem is also included in her poetry collection, *The Forest Of My Mind*, which was a Hot New Release for Canadian poetry books. The poem will also be part of a multi-media production that she is currently collaborating with artists on.

As a writer, storytelling is at the heart of everything Heidi Sander does. Her greatest joy is to foster the love of writing and to encourage others to share their stories and writing. Her online program, *"Pathways To Poetry"* holds that passion and is part of her larger vision for the poetry and literary community.

Website: www.heidisander.com
Facebook & Instagram: @heidisanderwriter

I am of this earth,
molecules of water
dripped from a leaf
into the mouth of a bird
evaporated to rain
dropping onto my tongue.

I am rooted
in this moment,
of open sky,
outstretched arms
cradling leaves
drifting thoughts
through me
like air,
I breathe myself
onto the page.

HEIDI SANDER

About Plants & Poetry

Plants & Poetry is a small woman and indigenous-owned business founded in Northwest Arkansas in 2019. Jamie Nix and Leslie Walker create a space that nurtures a love for the arts and science, offering poetry & plant education to reconnect with the soil and soul. Leslie Walker manages a Food Forest, The Oasis, in Bella Vista, where she hosts various workshops and events. Jamie Nix and her husband, Tariq Ait Lahouari operate a nature-inspired publication, *Plants & Poetry Journal*. For every submission received at the Journal, they plant a tree or type of vegetation in The Oasis. *Plants & Poetry Journal* publishes poetry, prose, mixed media, and creative nonfiction. Collections include "Art Meets Science, Examining Biodiversity & Conservation," "Seeing Synergies, A Two Species Interaction," "Gravity's Grave, Exploring Air, Water, & Soil," "Plant People, An Anthology of Environmental Artists," "Autumn Equinox Collection," "Wildlife of the Underworld," and upcoming collection, "my core rises: mycorrhiza collection." *Plants & Poetry Journal* has worked with over 100+ contributors, artists, writers, poets, scholars, and environmentalists worldwide.

Workshops include When Pens Bloom: A Regenerative Poetry, Prose Storytelling, Balcony Composting, Writing Poems For Your Plants, Playlists For Poetry, and Forest Therapy.

For more information, visit www.plantsandpoetry.org
Contact: plantsandpoetry.journal@gmail.com

About Pathways to Poetry

Pathways to Poetry is an interactive multimedia online program that helps emerging and established poets develop their writing, publish their poetry, and promote their work.

"We Are All Poets" is one of the foundational principles of each and every workshop and course Heidi Sander creates. She started the *Pathways to Poetry* program when she won her poetry award — she wanted to give back to the poetry community and offer poets an opportunity to learn from her experience. The program offers a supportive and safe environment in a private community where poets can explore their own writing.

The philosophy behind this program is to encourage every poet to explore and discover their poetic voice and all the possibilities it offers. The program starts with the foundational elements of poetry to ensure that the poet has deeply explored their own writing and then Heidi offers the many options for publishing and promotion that are open to a poet. For those seeking motivation, guidance, or accountability, the program can be transformational.

> "Pathways To Poetry is very well structured and it helped me learn new ways of expressing myself, developing further my creative mind by learning more about different writing techniques, and staying connected with fellow writers' work.

It also helped me stay organized and focused, kept me accountable, and gave me more self-confidence about my writing. It made me realize how important poetry is to me, it feeds my soul and heals my heart. I can't live without it. I have been writing poetry, on and off, my whole life, the course helped me get back on track."

– Donna Teodorov

For more information, visit www.heidisander.com or https://pages.heidisander.com/pathwaystopoetry/

CPSIA information can be obtained
at www.ICGtesting.com
Printed in the USA
BVHW030034070622
639031BV00008B/146